M000248069

ACKNOWLEDGEMENTS

In writing this workbook, I would like to thank Michelle Brown, Zaneta Lennon, Malcolm Wells, Patrice Lisbon, Olivette Moss, Shannon Whitehead, Chris Lennon, Rosa Ashe, Phillis Holliday, Rhonda Page and Linda Jiles for your support.

ISBN: 978-0-9743043-0-4

DEDICATION

I dedicate this workbook to the
memory of my mother:

Ramella Roberts Blalock

Go to our website to learn more
about using our video series while
completing your journal
activateyourbest.com/reinvent

Jessica Blalock, Ph.D., born in Atlanta, Georgia, is an Applied Psychologist. She is the Director of The Center for Discovery, INC, which offers creative books, videos and training that promote self-awareness and leadership.

Contents

INTRODUCTION

The purpose of this workbook is to guide you in the process of gaining a clear understanding about yourself and your individual journey. This workbook helps people of all backgrounds focus on (re)discovering, examining, and developing their emotional, mental, social, and physical selves. By (re)discovering yourself, you can improve your behavior, thinking and interactions with others by first making changes in yourself.

This workbook will assist you on the path to

- reflect (examine strengths, gaps, purpose, daily best practices)
- plan (clarify your focus)
- act (create a plan of action to reach desired and critical goals)

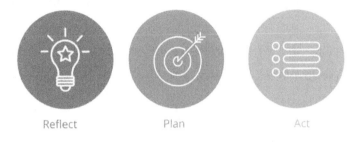

Reflect   Plan   Act

Discover Yourself!

Developing and nurturing yourself (spirit, body, and mind) is extremely important in your life. As a result of adverse emotions (e.g., depression, fear, greed, sadness, low self-esteem, hatred) that cause mental disturbances, people may behave in a manner that is not consistent with one's true self. This can get you off balance and you begin to neglect some parts of yourself including:

Reflect

Emotional: Allowing negative thoughts, attitudes, and behavior to impact your life

Mental Aspiration: Not following or pursuing activities related to your overall purpose in life

Social Relationships: Being more defensive and critical of family, friends, or co-workers

Exercise: Not exercising or taking care of your physical body

We must realize that we will not leave this world without the opportunity to gain experience and develop from multiple experiences. One question you may ask when feeling down or having aversive experiences is,

"Am I going to stay down or pick myself up?"

Are you going to make the same mistakes repeatedly? Are you going to blame others for your problems? Are you going to stay in the same negative environment that led to your current situation? Are you going to have the same self-defeating attitude?

Each individual controls the directions he takes in his life. The decisions you make will have an impact on your entire life. In essence, you are the only one who can save you! Often, we look outside ourselves for someone to save us, but change begins with you.

One essential factor of life is self-development. The Discover Yourself Model (see Figure 1) is unique because it focuses on developing the whole person. This approach attempts to develop individuals based on a holistic way of thinking that assumes individuals are spiritual beings that come into this world with some sort of spiritual base and purpose. This is different from many current developmental models of behavior that assume when individuals are born into the world, they are like blank slates. Some assume people learn from different stimuli once they develop and grow within their lives.

By going deep into yourself, learning from within, you engage in a reawakening process that supports as well as determines your life's purpose. Moreover, you establish a sense of who you are and assess your present and future roles. Once you have that sense, you begin to have more clarity about your personal and career-related goals and future aspirations. It is essential to note that although you may establish future short and long-term goals, the road to the desired point is individualistic and challenging. The process is individualistic because each person experiences things in unique ways. It is important to learn, grow and stay focused on those unique experiences. You must stay aligned with your overall goals and purpose in life. As things change in your life, your goals and purpose may also need to be modified.

This workbook is based on a model I created that has shown to successfully help people increase happiness, improve overall health and effectiveness in their personal and professional lives. This model postulates that in order for a person to be happy, healthy, and effective, there are key overlapping contributors.

- What you tune into regularly (Step 1- relaxation of the mind)
- The ability to take control of one's emotional, social, and physical self (Step 2 - emotions, social interactions, and physical body)
- The awareness and activation of key values, strengths, and purpose (Step 3 - aspirations)

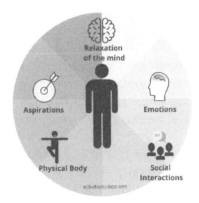

Figure 1: Discovery Yourself Model

Each component is broken down into one or more elements, specifically describing that component. The following provides a description of each component.

Mental - Relaxation of the mind: The Relaxation of the Mind component helps you get more in-tune with your inner self. The Relaxation of the Mind component examines how well you are tuning in to your inner self and principles and practices to help you clear your mind. This section reviews foundational activities that provides guidance and helps you manage stress or difficult situations.

Emotional: The Emotional component examines how you feel your thinking is influencing your development and how you see the world. Often, positive, or negative things that you focus on lead to actual outcomes or events within your life.

Social Interactions: The Social component examines your feelings about how you connect and communicate with others.

Physical Body: The Physical component reviews your diet, exercise habits and stress level. The elements within the Physical component examine how well you are caring for your physical body.

Values - Mental Aspiration: The Mental Aspiration component examines your values and purpose in life. This component gives you an opportunity to identify your personal values and helps you develop a purpose statement that explains what you are truly passionate about.

There is overlap between the Discover Yourself components. Positive or negative experiences you may have in one component can have an impact on your experiences in other components. For example:

- Getting in-tune helps you relax your physical body, manage your emotions, focus on your life's purpose
- Intense feelings can have an impact on the quality of your relationships
- Emotions can impact the functioning of your physical body
- Carrying out your life's work needs to be done in a state of emotional wellness. If not, this can lead to many unforeseen and unnecessary setbacks, limitations, and self-doubt

Strengths or weaknesses in one component can directly or indirectly affect another component. For example:

> David has been struggling to deal with his manager at work on a stressful job. His manager has given him a low performance appraisal rating for the past three years. Due to his low performance appraisal ratings, he is at risk of losing his job. He has tried on numerous occasions to communicate with his boss to discuss his performance; however, because of his boss's unfriendly attitude toward his employees, David has had a tough time communicating his feelings about his low appraisal ratings. For the past three years, David would take out his negative feelings (inability to communicate with his boss and his feelings of lack of control) on his wife and children. This occurred because he could not effectively communicate with his boss and he had a fear of losing his job at any time. In addition, he began to overload himself with negative emotions and thoughts about his boss and his job. This has impacted his physical health.

Getting to the root of a problem enables an individual to accurately assess and solve problems, not just the symptoms. Problems can cause one or more symptoms. You can often see the symptoms clearly, but not the source of the symptom (the source of the symptom is the problem). It can take some deep soul searching and/or counseling to get to the root of the problem.

David eventually went to a counselor and discovered he had a challenging time communicating with others. As a child, he was not able to voice his opinion and was often shunned by his parents. Once he learned how to communicate, he realized he was creating difficulties at work and at home.

When examining the whole person, you will be able to develop yourself, create desired circumstances and determine what you need to do to continue to develop yourself.

By assessing yourself within each component, you will have an opportunity to review the importance of each component and identify what can be done to help your growth and development for life. After reviewing each component, you will have the opportunity to answer questions about things that you are doing in your life to develop your life and what you feel you should be doing to improve the quality of your life.

Five Steps To Self-Discovery

Figure 2: Steps to Self-Discovery

The workbook is broken down into five steps. In each section, you will answer questions about your life's experiences and how to improve the quality of your life.

Step 1 helps you get in-tune with your inner self.

Step 2 helps you examine experiences relating to your emotional, physical, and social self. After reviewing each component, you will have the opportunity to answer questions about your emotional, physical, and social self; and examine what you feel you should be doing to improve the quality of your life.

Step 3 helps you clarify your personal values and life's purpose.

Step 4 provides behaviors, principles and practices that will help you change undesired behaviors and reach your goals.

Step 5 helps you create goals and take action on your desired goals. After creating your plan, continuously review it, stay focused and make changes as needed.

How to Use this Workbook

Before completing the exercises on the following pages, go to activateyourbest.com/reinvent to learn about the Discover Yourself video series. This series provides additional tools and resources to help you *Discover*, *Plan* and *Activate* your best Self with ease.

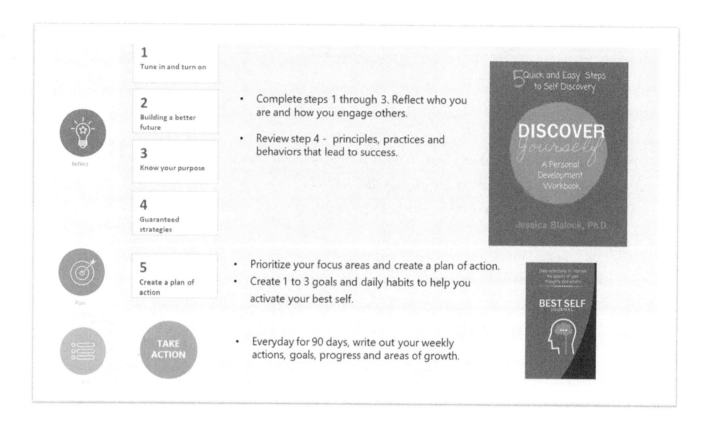

1
Tune in and Turn On

The first step to discover yourself is to get in-tune with your inner self. To get in tune with your inner self, let's review the Tune in and Turn on component.

Tuning in and turning on helps you connect to your inner self (e.g., your feelings, emotions, fantasies, intuition, values, beliefs, personality, desires, purpose). Who are you? What are your innate desires?

As a result of tuning into your inner self regularly, you can:
- better manage emotions, triggers, stress, and anxiety
- be more in tune to your core values

During the process of self-discovery, it is essential to focus inward to establish who you are and where you are going. When you take time to reflect and focus inward, it gives you the opportunity to concentrate on things that are happening in your life. This is the place you get answers to questions and make decisions about things that you are experiencing (are your thoughts, actions and behaviors aligned with your inner self?).

Connecting to your inner self can be done by relaxing and clearing the mind – Tuning in and Turning on.

The following section includes exercises that will help you reflect on how you get in tune with your inner self. We will review
- Deep breathing, gratitude, and mindfulness – recommended to practiced daily
- Additional activities to help you relax your physical mind

Tuning in and Turning on Activities

Deep Breathing

Taking deep breaths is the foundation of relaxing the physical mind and body. It is the foundation to many activities that help you relax such as gratitude, mindfulness, yoga, visualization and more. Deep breathing allows you to take in more oxygen and release more carbon dioxide. Take time to practice deep breathing throughout your day, especially during stress and engaging in activities that help you relax.

The following exercise shows you how to practice deep breathing. Practice deep breathing the first thing in the morning and throughout the day.

- Sit or lie down maintaining good posture. Make sure your body is relaxed and close your eyes.
- Pay attention to your breathing – and nothing else. Place one hand on the part of your chest or abdomen that seems to rise and fall the most with each breath.

Deep breathing helps you calm your mind and relax in the present moment.

- Place both hands on your abdomen and follow your breathing, noticing how your abdomen rises and falls.
- Breathe in through your nose or mouth. Make sure your chest is moving in harmony with your abdomen.
- Now place one hand on your abdomen and one hand on your chest.
- Inhale deeply and slowly through your nose into your abdomen. You should feel your abdomen rise with this inhalation and your chest should move only a little.
- Pay attention to the space between your inhale and exhalation.
- Exhale through your mouth or nose, keeping your mouth, tongue, and jaw relaxed.
- Relax as you focus on the sound and feeling of long, slow, deep breaths.

Deep breaths can be taken to release resistance to feeling good and allowing other things into your vibrations.

Live in Gratitude

Deep breathing and expressing feelings of gratitude throughout the day increases happiness, helps you get through tough times, and it can simply rewire your brain.

Being gratitude focused is about being appreciative and focusing on good things and blessings of life. Life is filled with ups and downs, highs, and lows. Be grateful for and reflect on

- what you have learned from previous situations
- wonderful things that have occurred in your life
- things you have done to help other people and
- simple things that make your life easy.

Often, we focus more on what we need and desire, and take little time to focus on good things, lessons learned and accomplishments. Remember, focusing your mind on lack, leads to lack and limitations; focusing your mind on opportunities and growth, leads to opportunities and growth.

On your life's journey, show gratitude for the blessings and the pitfalls of your journey. Being gratitude focused helps you create a mindset of abundance.

Express Gratitude for...
- family and friends
- your accomplishments
- managers/co-workers
- food, shelter and water
- past mistake
- your job
- people you see, meet, and think about
- things that have occurred within the last 24 hours
- growth opportunities
- someone who has helped you achieve a goal
- your health
- music you love
- simple things in life
- your past
- a mentor or teacher
- a book you enjoyed
- the city you live in
- your favorite holiday

activateyourbest.com

Write down five things you are grateful for **today**. Who or what are you grateful for? What are some blessings that have occurred within your life that you are most proud of?

I am so grateful for...

I can show more gratitude, by doing the following...

Think of someone who has helped you achieve something within the past week. Send them a thank you card to show your appreciation.

Mindfulness

Often, people are buried in thoughts about the past, planning the future or simply engaged in the stresses of the day. But what if you allow yourself five minutes (or more) a day to pay attention to the present. Specifically, turn off the television and personal devices. By doing this, you are engaging in the practice of **mindfulness.**

According to the Jon Kabat-Zinn (a famous teacher of mindfulness), mindfulness is:

"...PAYING ATTENTION IN A PARTICULAR WAY...ON PURPOSE, IN THE PRESENT MOMENT, AND NONJUDGMENTALLY."

Overall, mindfulness is stilling your mind and bringing yourself to the present moment, without judgment and being open to experiences as they come. Being mindful helps you direct your attention on a person, an object, or your breath. It is being fully present to each moment while spending less time concerned about what is going on around us. It is easily understood, and it requires no major training.

Mindfulness is available every moment of the day and can be practiced anywhere. Take short pauses throughout the day to engage in the practice of mindfulness. While practicing mindfulness, reflect on the smell, taste, sound or feel of these activities.

Mindfulness also helps you recognize your intentions. Your intentions are how you direct your attention. What are your thoughts focused on? What are you grateful for? Knowing your intentions enables you to have more clarity about your aims and goals.

Benefits

APA (2012) revealed there are many benefits of engaging in the practice of mindfulness. Here are a few.
- reduces stress
- decreases anxiety and depression – living in the past and future increases it
- improves memory and performance at work
- increases the skill of self-observation
- helps people respond to relationship stress
- increases happiness

Here are some ways you can be more mindful (paying attention to the present without judgement)
- cloud gaze – watch the clouds move and rest
- listen to birds sounds - notice the quality of the sound
- pay attention as you are eating - eat slowly without distractions (observe smells, sounds, textures, flavors and how the food makes you feel)

In summary, pay attention to the present moment. Practice experiencing sights, sounds taste, and smells without labeling them. When you notice your mind is distracted, without judgement, bring it back to your experience.

Engaging in these short pauses throughout the day can benefit your emotional and physical health and improve your relationships with others.

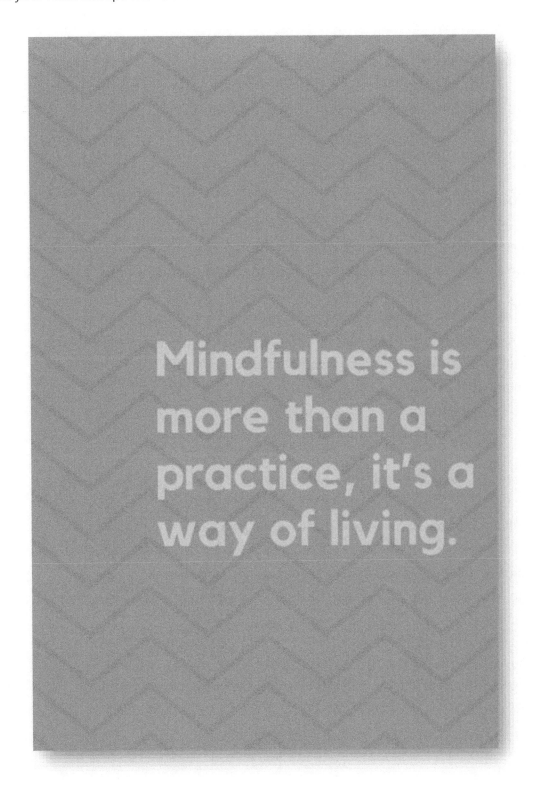

Mindfulness is more than a practice, it's a way of living.

Tune in and Turn on Activities

The following lists additional activities to foster the process of getting in-tune with your Self. These activities can help change undesired thoughts, behavior, and circumstances.

Meditation: *Mindfulness is the awareness of something whereas meditation is the awareness of nothing.* According to Ashby (1997), meditation is defined as the practice of mental exercises that allows the meditator to have control over the mind by stopping vibrations of the mind due to undesired thoughts, imaginations, etc.

Meditation allows you to get in-tune to your inner self. It can help you
- clear your mind
- improve memory and attention span
- reduce stress and anxiety
- overcome procrastination

Once you begin to relax, make sure your mind is clear. This may take several meditation sessions because when you first start meditating you may have many things go through your head.

To meditate, take fifteen minutes or more each day to quietly reflect on your life. Meditate in a quiet place where you are alone, such as a bedroom, bathroom, park, etc. Sit in a position that feels comfortable or natural to you. Take several deep breaths, inhale through your mouth and exhale through your nose or mouth.

Taking deep breaths help you decrease tension, increase energy, and promote health.

This can be done every day. Meditating daily for a certain period of time will lead to an experience of inner peace. You may forget your existence and have a sensation of floating. You will less likely become angered at things that you normally would have in the past.

Yoga: Yoga is the union of the mind, body, and spirit. Yoga creates inner harmony, improves flexibility and physical and mental health. Yoga can be done a few minutes a day to produce a calming state and a cheerful outlook. According to Burton Goldberg (1999):

> *"The concept behind the study of yoga is the integration of the mind and body, explained by the observation that when the mind is restless and agitated, the health of the body will be adversely affected and when the body is ill, mentally functioning will be comprised."*

Prayer: Prayer is giving thanks and asking for guidance within your life. It is important to be specific in what you ask for and pray for a specific solution. Thereafter, give thanks knowing that your prayers are affirmed.

Affirmations: Affirmations are statements about your thoughts and emotions that create the energy of what you desire. Affirmations should always be positive and specific. Having consistent or ongoing negative thoughts or feelings about something can become reality.

Saying positive affirmations can help direct your attention so you will create positive thoughts about a specific behavior or situation. You can write, say, or sing your desires. There are examples of affirmations later in the book.

Visualization: Visualization is forming a mental concept about things that you desire to happen. You can begin to visualize what you desire by imagining yourself doing or being what you are working toward. Imagine you are self-engaging in the activity that you wish to accomplish. Make sure you visualize what you want on a regular basis and have the intention to achieve what you are visualizing!

Rituals: Rituals are a detailed method of procedure faithfully or regularly followed. It is important to develop rituals at the same time and the same place each day.

Centering Yourself Inventory

The following questions will help you reflect on your strengths and gaps regarding tuning in.

- How often do you get in tune to your inner self?
- What activities do you engage in to get in tune to your inner self?
- How does it make you feel?

- How satisfied are you with your level of relaxing your mind on a regular basis?
- What can you do differently?

Go to page 93 and write the centering activities you are satisfied with and centering activities you want to incorporate within your life.

Guiding Principles

Guiding principles provide a framework for carrying out behavior. Following specific principles help us stay focused and aligned to our values and the guidance we received while Tuning in and Turning On. Let's review a few principles that are important to incorporate in your life daily.

PATIENCE

Patience is waiting or being delayed and being OK with this process.
- Understand situations may alter
- Continuously persevere after hardship
- Being calm during a storm
- Have a willingness to tolerate delay

COURAGE

Having courage is about having the tenacity to stand up for what you know is right.
- Being brave
- Facing ones fears
- Confidently standing up for what you believe in
- Taking responsibility for mistakes and areas of growth

FORGIVENESS

Forgiveness is forgiving yourself and others for something that has occurred in the past.
- Letting go of past/current hurts or pains
- Being at peace with the past and focusing on the present and the future
- Accepting yourself as a human who has faults and makes mistakes
- Living in the present and accepting the past

COMPASSION

Compassion shows that you are aware and knowledgeable of pain a person may face as a result of their life experiences. Compassion can be built by having compassionate visualizations and wishes during meditation practices.
- Make an effort to learn something about friends/ colleagues such as interests, hobbies or major life events
- Sense others emotions and try to understand their perspective
- Have a genuine concern for others

INTEGRITY

Integrity is living a life of truth and being honest to yourself and others.
- Communicate information accurately
- Carry out personal commitments
- Follow through on agreements - practice what you preach
- Acknowledge mistakes or limitations

FAITH

Faith is to believe in something of a higher nature, even when the outlook appears dim.
- Having the willpower to believe in something that far exceeds your expectations
- Maintaining harmony with your inner self
- Believing in something of a higher nature

Answer the following questions regarding guiding principles.

What principles do you follow on a regular basis and why?
What could you say or do more of to incorporate one or more of the principles listed in your life?

Go to page 93 and write the principles you are satisfied with and what needs to be improved.

2 Building a Better Future

Now that we have reviewed the foundation to relaxing your mind and gaining insights, let's review Step 2: Building a Better Future. This step helps you examine:

- how your thinking leads to current experiences-- Take Control of Your Thoughts
- your interactions with others--Take Control of What You Say
- your diet, how often do you exercise, and your stress level--Take Control of Your Physical Body

Take Control of Your Thoughts

The Emotional component examines how your thinking influences your future experiences and your development. Figure 3 explains how thinking leads to actual experiences.

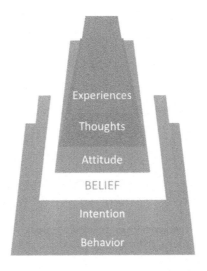

Figure 3: Emotional Concept Theory

The emotional concept theory assumes that experiences are shaped from conception to adulthood and influenced by cultural norms. There are many factors that have an impact on your emotions and behavior such as your mother's experiences while carrying you through birth, parental upbringing, education, environment, place of birth, etc. This model postulates the following.

- *Cultural norms are perceptions of what you feel you should do based on culture, family and/or friends*
- *Cultural norms influence how you perceive experiences*
- *Past experiences lead to thoughts, unconscious and conscious*
- *Thoughts lead to attitudes that are positive or negative feelings about behavior*
- *Attitudes lead to beliefs; beliefs lead to intentions*
- *Intentions lead to behavior*

Thus, our own individual experiences represent our unique experience we have on earth. An example of the model is:

> *Renee consumed a lot of alcohol during her pregnancy with her daughter Leslie. In addition, she did not want to have her baby. Renee gave birth to Leslie, who grew up in a non-loving environment. As a baby, Leslie cried a lot because she rarely received attention from her mother and no one else was around. In addition, as Leslie got older, her mother still had an alcohol dependency. Renee neglected her child throughout her development by putting her down all the time, telling her she would never accomplish anything and emotionally abusing Leslie. Leslie created beliefs that she was not loveable, good enough and everything was her fault. Leslie eventually grew up and had low self-esteem, fear of failure, suffered from drug and alcohol dependency and made low grades in school.*

Your past experiences and intentions lead to future experiences. It is important that Leslie examine herself (possibly with the help of a counselor or therapist) and her experiences to determine why her life is in its current situation. Here are some things that may help Leslie heal as she goes on the path of healing herself. Specifically, Leslie can:

- Talk to a counselor or friend and reveal her experiences that have led her to where she is now. She can also write down her experiences (journaling) and how her experiences made her feel.
- Forgive her mother and herself (this is a process). It may also help if Leslie determines the type of childhood her mother had that led her mother to be who she is today (empathy). Then she may begin to understand why her mother is the way she is.
- Write affirmations saying she forgives her mother totally and unconditionally.
- Visualize herself accomplishing certain goals and having loving experiences with her mother.

Here is an example of how the model works.

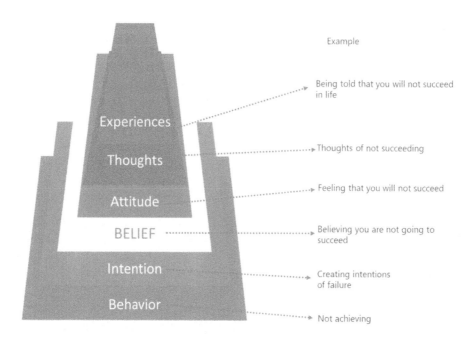

Emotions have an impact on the functioning and overall condition of internal organs. Based on Eastern centered philosophies, it is speculated that each emotion is linked to a specific organ within the body. More recently, Western holistic teaching started emphasizing this in the mind and body connection. According to Wright:

> *Grief is linked with the lungs and through them can affect the heart. Worry can reduce lung energy and lead to breathlessness and feelings of anxiety. Overwork puts a strain on the spleen, reducing its ability to keep the digestive system working at peak efficiency. Shock causes a sudden drop in heart chi (energy) - - with direct effects of the heart such as palpations – but can reduce kidney energy. Anger can create an excess of liver energy, causing headaches and dizziness. Long-term anger (which can take the form of nagging resentment, frustration and even depression, as well as the more obvious irritability) can make this excessive liver energy interfere with the spleen's work of protecting the digestive system (1999).*

Louise Hay (1999) developed an extensive list (about forty-six pages) of health problems and probable emotional causes linked to the problems. This model postulates that thinking in a negative direction can lead to negative future experiences and/or disease within the physical body.

Thus, it is important to attempt to assess your thoughts and focus them in a positive direction.

The following section includes exercises that will help you reflect on how you manage your thoughts and emotions. This section includes activities that will guide you through the self-awareness process and activities that can help you identify and get rid of undesired thoughts and feelings.

In this section, you will review
- What I like about myself
- Past experiences
- Limiting beliefs
- Triggers

Take Control of Your Thoughts Activities

1	2	3	4	5	6	7	8	9	10

Not at all satisfied   *Extremely satisfied*

What I Like About Myself

In this section, write what you like and dislike about yourself?

Five or more things I <u>like</u> about myself are:

Five or more things I <u>dislike</u> about myself are:

Reflect on the Past

In this section, reflect on experiences that you have had in the past. Determine how these experiences have impacted your life.

- Reflect on 1-4 experiences that you have had in the past that have helped you get to where you are today. How has this molded you into the person that you are now or continue to mold you into the person you aspire to be?

*Experiences that have occurred throughout your life that have shaped your life.	What did you learn from this experience?	What would you change if you had to do it again?	How has this improved the quality of your life?

*Experiences with family, friends, co-workers, church members, teachers, etc.

*Experiences that have occurred throughout your life that have shaped your life.	What did you learn from this experience?	What would you change if you had to do it again?	How has this improved the quality of your life?

Identifying Limiting Beliefs

BELIEFS	Negative	Positive
Love	• I don't matter • People don't care about me • I am unlikeable, unwanted	• I am acceptable • I am loveable • I matter
Defective	• I am powerless/helpless • I am a failure • Everything is my fault	• I can accomplish what I set out to accomplish • I did my best • Mistakes help me learn faster • I can safely let go of some control
Worthy	• I am worthless • I am broken/damaged • I am hurtful/dangerous	• I am ok just as I am • I can accept myself • I am good enough
Value	• I should not be here at all • People take me for granted • People reject me	• I am important • I am significant • I am deserving
Guilt	• I am stupid • I am flawed • I am shameful • I should be punished	• I can learn from my mistakes • I did my best • I trust that I am where i need to be • I am deserving even when I make mistakes
Abandonment	• I am not important • People I love will leave me • No one can be trusted	• I am important • I can get my needs met • I am supported
Entitlement	• I am worthless if I don't succeed • I am entitled to special treatment • I must be respected • People should be the way I expect them to be	• I can easily let go of the past • I treat others with respect, compassion and gratitude • I do not compare myself to others • I celebrate others success even when I feel like a failure

Reflection. Write down one <u>Negative</u> belief you have about yourself? What experiences helped shape this belief? Determine when this belief arises in your thoughts or feelings? How does it make you feel?

Throughout the week, spend time reflecting on and writing down your negative and positive beliefs. For Negative beliefs, write down what you can do to change this belief.

Identifying Triggers

Now that you have reflected on past experiences and your beliefs, identify your triggers on the next page. Triggers are a reminder of past anxieties or traumas or they may be brought on by something that is inconsistent with your values (you will identify your values in step 3). To identify your triggers

- Think of a situation where you were "set off" inappropriately.
- Visualize the situation. What happened right before you got upset? How did you feel?
- Finally, create potential solutions that would help you manage your triggers.

Reflection	Feeling	Outcome	Story	Potential Solutions
Reflect. Determine what caused your trigger	How did you feel? Where did you feel the emotion in your body?	Notice what you said to yourself and others Were there key phrases?	What is your story? Why did this cause an emotional/physical reaction?	• Create a strategy to help eliminate or limit the trigger. • Determine what you can do differently? Is there a new direction to take?
Example				
Getting negative feedback from a manager/mentor	**Underlying beliefs –** defective/not good enough **Emotions** – Anger, disappointment, see chart online **Physical Body** – (racing heartbeat, shortness of breath, lost train of thought)	Oversharing, freezing, becoming argumentative, gossiping, blaming	I do not feel I am good enough. When my mentor/ manager looks at me in a disapproving way, I remember that this is the way my mother looked at me often. Nothing I did was good enough	Before this trigger occurs again, I will... • Work on my self-confidence • When I feel angry I will, take deep breaths, focus on solutions, and not gossip – I will seek advice from someone I trust • Say affirmations regularly such as I am capable and qualified for this role or I am enough

Reflection	Feeling	Outcome	Story	Potential Solutions

Now that you have completed, Take Control of Your Thoughts, Go to page 93 and write down what you do well and what you can start doing to help you take control of your thoughts (potential categories – being aware of one's emotions, managing emotions (e.g., stress, controlling impulses, self-motivation), being more empathetic, being more self-confident)

Take Control of What You Say

Do you have the right people around you – close and extended relationships? Do you effectively communicate your thoughts? The social component helps you reflect on your circles of influence and how you communicate with others.

Social interactions occur from the time a person is born until death. Over time, these interactions shape behavior. Social interactions with others are an important part of human development. Human beings are naturally social creatures.

Sometimes our relationships with others (e.g., co-workers, spouse, family, and friends) can be challenging because of personality conflict, negative emotions (these negative emotions may arise because of jealousy, fear, resentment, etc.) or poor communication skills.

It is important to have various layers of social circles to help you navigate through life and life's challenges. People within these circles help us reduce stress, solve problems, manage emotions, and increase motivation for success. Developing and maintaining positive relationship with others and clarifying boundaries (who you should share personal thoughts and feelings with) can affect our development and overall feelings.

Let's review important circles of influence and who should be in these circles.

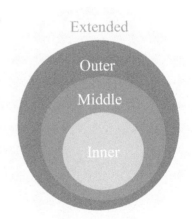

Inner circle

- o People you trust, share your inner private thoughts with.
- o People who are always there for you. There is mutual support.
- o People you trust and turn to when problems arise.
- o People you have deep connections with.
- o People who hold you accountable, are authentic and honest.
- o The number of people in this circle is typically less than 6 people.
- o Staying in touch with them regularly is important.

- Middle circle
  - o People you enjoy being around, have similar experiences and interests.
  - o These people are usually family, mentors, and best friends.
  - o People you spend time with and share experiences and stories.
  - o You do not share private, intimate details with people in your middle circle.
  - o Show up for these people when it matters most.
  - o Move in and out of this circle based on common activities and interests.

- o The number of people in this circle varies.

- Outer circle
    - o People you share interest with at work, community, and some family members.
    - o Casual relationships with people you are friendly with.
    - o People you communicate with occasionally.
    - o This circle is open – people come in and out as things change.
    - o The number of people in this circle varies.
    - o In your outer circle, you do not spend a lot of time with, invest a lot of emotion, and share intimate private thoughts or feelings with people in this circle.

- Extended
    - o People you are around but there is no or low trust.
    - o The number of people in this circle varies.
    - o This group includes coworkers, some family friends, neighbors, and people you communicate with on social media

Take Control of What You Say Activities

In this section, describe your relationships with people in your inner, middle, outer, and extended circles. List the steps you can take to improve these relationships.

What is your satisfaction level with your interacting with others?

1	2	3	4	5	6	7	8	9	10

Not at all satisfied   *Extremely satisfied*

Circles of Influence

Name the people in your circles (e.g., family, friends, spouse, co-workers, community)? For groups, list the names of the groups (not the individuals in the groups).

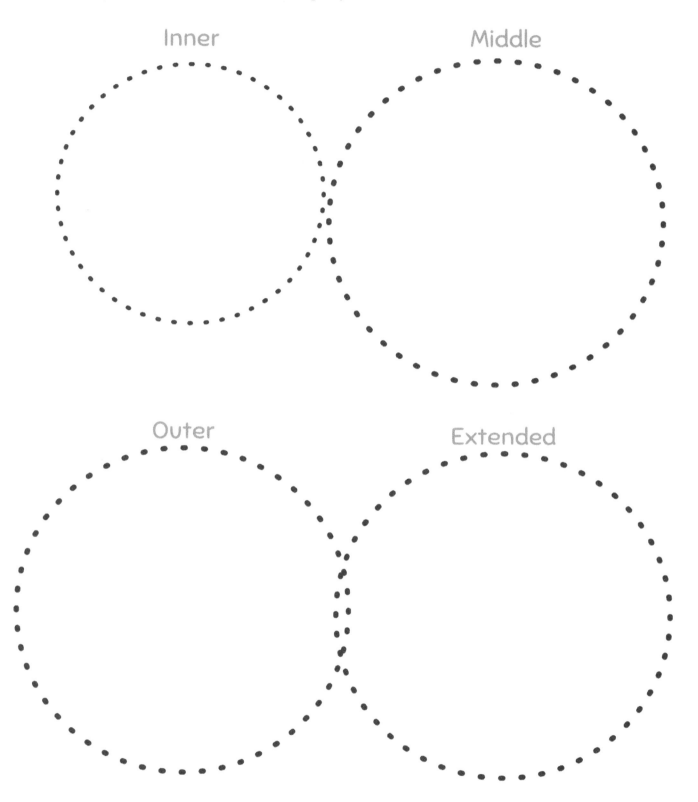

Inner

Middle

Outer

Extended

Reflect on the people in your circles. Is everyone in the right circle? If not, move them to the correct circle.

Are you doing and saying the right things to people in your circles (for example, do you share more personal information with people in your inner circles and less information with people in your outer circles)? On this page, write down what you can do differently to effectively communicate with people in your circles.

Actively Listening to Others

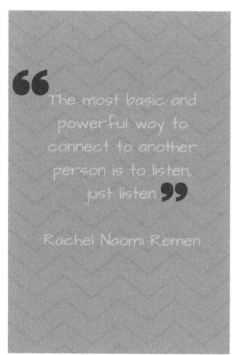

> The most basic and powerful way to connect to another person is to listen, just listen.

Rachel Naomi Remen

How well do you listen to people in your circles? Do you sometimes wait and listen to what someone is saying and not attentively listen to what is being said? When you listen actively you focus your full attention on the person who is speaking. You can ask good questions, practice compassion and empathy, and listen without judgment.

Let's review some important aspects of listening.

Respect. Active listening shows you respect the person who is talking, and you are genuinely interested in what they have to say. Your level of listening might fluctuate depending on how interested you are in the conversation. However, if you are a part of a conversation, show respect and attentively listen to the message.

Mindfulness. When listening to others, allow your mind to be clear and quiet. Listen without judgement, criticism, or interruption. Soak in as much information as you can and listen for understanding rather than thinking about what you are going to say or thinking with judgment.

Compassion. Display compassion when listening. Being compassionate is to have and maintain a sensitivity to others feelings about something. As a result of being compassionate, you can be more open to listening to other people's views. Showing compassion or empathizing with others doesn't mean you agree with their point of view; however, it shows that you recognize the process of life that everyone is different with different viewpoints. You cannot change other people; the only person you can change is yourself.

Recognize differences. When communicating with others, recognize that people are different, coming from distinct cultures, background, personality, or experiences. That means we may have different perspectives, simply because we come from different walks of life.

Someone in China may have a separate way of expressing themselves and have different cultural experiences and expectations than someone from America. Someone in your family may have a different definition of family than you do.

Reflection. Active listening helps you learn something new about yourself and the person(s) you are talking to. You can reflect on what you can learn from this situation, or how you can help others or yourself by experiencing this. Or you can determine this is not someone I should continue to be around or communicate with.

Communicating with Others

What we say to others shows information about our personality, dispositions, and personal style. It also reveals our emotional state of wellness and love for others.

> *Speaking words of hate and malice brings us to a point that derails our state of Love, thereby impacting others and ourselves. Speaking words of kindness and compassion emphasizes our state of Love.*

We all communicate our thoughts, words, and deeds to others in some form. When communicating, turn on your guiding principles, as discussed in the previous chapter *Tune in and Turn On*. Determine if the words you speak, and your tone are reflective of these principles. The principles are:

- patience
- courage
- forgiveness
- compassion
- courage

Although these principles can be reflected in the words you speak, also recognize that you are a unique individual. Sometimes, people automatically think others should think like them or process information as they would. Because you think one thing is normal, or a correct process, doesn't mean someone else thinks it is a normal or correct process as well. Everyone is unique with different personalities, values, strengths, and interests.

To practice active listening skills and communicating with others, review the tips in step 4. Then go to Appendix A and B and complete the exercises.

Listening and Communication Activity

How do you get your point across to people in your circles? Reflect on your communication strengths and areas of development.

What are your communication strengths (e.g., listening, speaking, nonverbal)?

What are your communication areas of development (e.g., listening, speaking, nonverbal)?

Think about how you communicate with others. Are you satisfied with getting your point across to others? Are you satisfied with taking control of what you say? If not, list five ways you can improve your communication.

Go to page 93 and write the communication skills and "circles of influence" you are satisfied with and what you need to improve or develop.

"Kind Words Can Be Short And Easy To Speak, But Their Echoes Are Truly Endless."

Mother Theresa

Take Control of Your Physical Body

The physical body houses the spirit and inside your physical body are your emotions (i.e., thoughts, feelings, beliefs, and attitude).

These components make each individual unique. Your physical body will remain with you throughout your life on Earth and will separate from your spirit at death. As a result, loving, respecting, taking care of, and accepting the physical body is important in your development.

The Physical Body component includes diet, exercise, and stress. This component examines your typical diet (including health challenges), exercises or sports in which you engage and how you respond in stressful situations.

Diet, exercise, and stress have a direct link to the overall health and well-being of your physical body. When your physical body is not functioning properly, of course, it affects other components.

The Physical Body component allows you to reflect on how well you feel you are taking care of your body and what you can do to develop healthy practices in this area. Often, due to our busy schedules, we feel we do not have enough time to exercise or eat right. As a result, we neglect our bodies. By neglecting our bodies, we may have less energy because we have not given our body the fuel it needs to perform effectively.

The following section includes exercises that will help you reflect on how you take care of your physical body through diet, exercise, and stress.

Take Control of Your Physical Body Activities

Dietary Habits Review

Nurturing your body through food has an impact on your psyche. Remember:

"You are what you eat" and "What you put into your body is what you get out."

As a result, be cautious of the types of foods you put into your body. There are many different theories that advocate what types of food may be good for your body. Currently, the typical American diet includes an excess of contaminated and over-processed foods.

Contaminated and over-processed foods have shown to cause toxicity in the body that leads to poor health and disease. Foods can become contaminated because of pesticides sprayed on fruits and vegetables. Andrew Weill explained that:

> *Standards for acceptable levels of toxic agrochemicals in foods are based on risks of acute toxicity—the possibility that exposure will cause immediate harm. They do not consider the risks of long-term cumulative damage to body defense and healing ability... those who argue that these chemical toxins are inconsequential to health fail to consider the possibility of synergy among them -- that the effects of exposure to multiple toxins might together cause real harm (1997).*

I am not promoting a specific diet. However, eating a variety of fresh unrefined organic foods such as fruits, vegetables (raw, lightly steamed, or broiled), grains, raw seeds and nuts, beans and some selected meats and fish (such as deep-water fish), allows the cells to absorb the energy produced by enzymes and provides the body with needed vitamins and minerals.

The following section helps you reflect on activities that can help you reflect on your dietary habits. This section gives you the opportunity to think about your health and dietary habits and steps you can take to make improvements.

Remember, this exercise is for your overall health. What you think needs to change to improve your diet may be based on recommendations from your doctor and your instincts about what you know is best for your body!

- Do you have any major or minor health problems? If yes, what are they?
- For how long?
- What impact does this have on your work/personal life?

- Do your parents have any major or minor health challenges?
- For how long?

What does a typical meal look like for you? Write down what you ate yesterday (or a typical day) (breakfast, lunch, dinner, and snacks).

Breakfast	Lunch	Dinner	Snacks

Exercise Review

Exercise is an activity that requires physical exertion of the muscles to keep the organs in a healthy state. Exercise has shown to improve digestion, elimination, keep your body in shape, burn fat, increase energy levels, and reduce stress. Keeping the blood circulating and stretching unused muscles help the physical functioning of the body. Exercise should not be viewed as something you have to do but something that you enjoy.

When developing your exercise regime, it is essential to make your regime specific to your body and what you can handle because individuals have different tolerance levels.

Often, people do not take time to engage in some sort of exercise practice because they may not be motivated or feel that they do not have time.

In this section, list your exercise practices and actions you can take to develop more rigorous exercise practices.

Activities to Engage in

Aerobics	Racquetball
Baseball	Rowing
Basketball	Running
Biking	Skiing
Body	Skating
Building	Soccer
Dance	Swimming
Fencing	Tae Bo
Golf	Tennis
Gymnastics	Track
Hiking	Volleyball
Karate	Walking

Answer the following questions about your current exercise regime.

- What types of exercise do you engage in? How often?
- Are you consistent with your exercise regime?
- What can you do differently to improve your exercise regime?

Stress Management Review

People encounter stress in emotionally disruptive situations. Stress can be caused by tension at work, problems paying bills, driving a car in traffic, tension in relationships with loved ones, new marriage, etc. Stress may cause tightened muscles, exhaustion, or physical pains (e.g., headaches, ulcers, depression). Stress usually affects parts of the body related to the nervous system, especially the digestive organs. If stress is not effectively managed, it can lead to illness within the body and reduce the quality of life.

Since stress can have a negative impact on the physical body, emotions, and social interactions, learning how to effectively manage and deal with stressful situations is essential in your life. There are a variety of approaches that may alleviate stress: meditation, visualization, yoga, deep breathing exercises, etc. (Review Step 1). Stress usually affects parts of the body related to the nervous system, especially the digestive organs. If stress is not effectively managed, it can lead to illness within the body and reduce one's quality of life.

Take Control of Your Thoughts helped you identify triggers, which can cause stress. In this section, review one thing that has caused you stressed within the last month (e.g., divorce, loss of job, family, job).

- What is one thing that has caused you stressed within the last month? How did it impact your physical body?
- How did you handle the stress?
- What could you have done differently?

Go to page 93 and write down what you are satisfied with and what you need to improve or develop regarding your diet, exercise, and how you manage stress.

3

Know Your Purpose

Know your purpose is the third step to discover yourself. This step includes the component mental aspirations – what you aspire to do and be within your life. In this section, list your strengths, values, life's purpose, and motto.

Reflect on who you are and how you can contribute to your family, your community and the world.

People can activate their best by being purpose focused. That is knowing your purpose and putting it to work in your life. When a person is not living or in a process of activating their true life's purpose, they can become isolated, have no will to live and feel depressed - especially in times of change or transition.

Purpose

Your purpose is something you are passionate about; it is who you are and what makes you unique. Purpose helps you determine the contributions you can make to your family, community, and/or the world. People who are clear about their purpose are generally more excited about life and their individual journal.

You can discover your personal power when you engage in behavior and activities that are related to your life's purpose.

Your purpose is not your job; although, it can be activities that you engage in at work or in your spare time with family, friends, or community.

Your purpose may change as you develop and grow in your life. If you do not engage in your purpose, you can often feel lifeless, depressed, or angry.

Knowing and activating your purpose can help raise your personal power because you will be focused on your life's work and doing what you love to do. Everyone has a unique role in the contribution to society. Through knowing and activating your purpose, you can discover your innate sense of being and recognize your unique gifts and contributions. Once you clarify your purpose, determine what you can do to make an impact. Do not just talk and think about it; engage in activities that will help you activate your true purpose.

Recently, I met with a client who was not clear about her purpose. She said she will engage her purpose as soon as she gets more money. This is very limiting because we do not know what tomorrow holds. Sometimes people get unfocused because they feel they know their purpose; however, they do not have the resources or means to carry it out. Remain focused and think of creative ways you can act out your purpose such as volunteering or participating in extra activities at work or at home.

Thus, no matter your situation, take time to activate your purpose on a regular basis. For example, if your purpose is to help others create a life of love and compassion, you can integrate behaviors and actions of love and compassion at work, with your family, church, or community.

Becoming purpose focused also requires turning on relaxation exercises such as mindfulness, yoga, and deep breathing (discussed in step 1 Tune in and Turn on). These activities will guide you in increasing your focus and commitment.

Purpose Statement

Your purpose statement clarifies your internal desires that are reflective of what you value in life and what you aim to be.

Knowing your true purpose can help you focus on your life's work and activate your passion. To help you create your purpose statement, you may ask yourself:

- What excites me about the world?
- What do I want to contribute to the world? Is it helping or teaching others, spending time with family, establishing, and maintaining a business or organizing events?

PURPOSE STATEMENT

Your purpose statement clarifies your internal desires that are reflective of what you value in life and what you aim to be.

Once your purpose is clear, it can be activated at work, your personal life or both.

The next few pages provide an opportunity for you to reflect and think about your true purpose. As a result, you will be clear about your important values, strengths, and purpose. In addition, you can record your purpose in the journal **Best Self** at activateyourbest.com/reinvent.

My Accomplishments/Successes

On the next few pages, write down all your major accomplishments. What are you good at? What are your greatest successes? Your accomplishments are your greatest achievements in your personal and professional life. Make sure you review old documents, awards, your resume, certificates, volunteer achievements, LinkedIn, etc.

My Sources of Inspiration

On the next page, write down who or what inspires you and how you inspire others. Here are some questions you can ask yourself.

- What people have inspired you in the past? Why?
- What leadership models or frameworks do you practice or integrate into your professional and personal life?
- How do you inspire other people?
- What can people expect from you? How do you set an example?

71

My Values and Strengths

Today, take time to clarify your values (what you care about) and your strengths (what you do well).

Values

To help you determine your purpose, knowing your values are important. Values are important things in your life that you care about based on your beliefs and convictions. Values are established because of years and years of experience and can truly be discovered under pressure.

Assessing your values will help determine the basis for your low or high motivation and can determine the origin of conflict with others. Many people who pursue work that is congruent with their values feel satisfied and successful in their life.

Here are questions to help you determine your core values
- What excites you the most?
- What makes you angry or upset?
- What are you most proud of?
- What things or events excites you the most?

To determine your most important values, think about a time when you were under stress or pressure. Did you use this value or forget about it? Under pressure, people determine what is important to them. If you have a clear set of values before a crisis, you are more prepared to make decisions based on the established values because you live by them and practice them every day.

Once you are clear about your important values, you can talk to people you interact with about their core values. Do you have the same core values as people you interact with? How are other people's values like your values? How are they different? As a result of knowing others important values, you will be better able to align yourself with others and it helps you understand why people do what they do.

When you identify your values, make sure other people around you are clear about what is important to you at work and in your personal life.

Strengths

After you have determined your values, identify your strengths. Your strengths are passions, talent, or skills that you excel in.

You can identify your strengths by:

- reviewing assessments (e.g., strengths, personality) you have taken in the past
- asking people you trust or people you work with to identify what you do well (often, people you are around have a clearer view of your strengths than you do)
- reflecting on fun times and times you were successful
- reflecting on things you are naturally good at doing

On the next two pages, circle all your important values and strengths. Then, write down the top five values and top five strengths that are important to you today in the journal **Best Self** (Best Self Profile Pages 10-11).

Acceptance
Abundance
Accountability
Achievement
Adaptability
Adventure
Ambition
Attention to Detail
Balance
Beauty
Commitment
Calmness
Caring
Challenge
Change
Charity
Cheerful
Comfort
Commitment
Community
Compassion
Competition
Concern for Others
Consciousness
Courage
Creativity
Customer Satisfaction
Discovery
Diversity
Dedication
Dominance
Education
Excellence
Fairness
Faith
Family
Flexibility
Focus
Freedom
Friendship
Giving
Honesty
Humility
Imagination
Independence

Individuality
Innovative
Integrity
Intelligence
Intuitive
Joy
Justice
Kindness
Knowledge
Leadership
Learning
Love
Loyalty
Organization
Patience
Persistence
Personal Growth
Philanthropy
Prosperity
Power
Professionalism
Quality
Relationships
Reliable
Resilience
Respect
Risk Taking
Safety
Security
Self-Awareness
Sense of Humor
Sensitivity
Service
Sharing
Sincerity
Spirituality
Spontaneous
Stability
Strength
Success
Sympathy
Teamwork
Thankful
Thorough
Thoughtful

Timely
Tolerance
Transparency
Trust
Truth
Unity
Vitality
Warmth
Wealth
Wisdom

Values

Activity
After you have identified your values, go to the section Triggers, in Step 2 – Take Control of Your Thoughts.
Reflect on each trigger and determine if one or more of your triggers was sparked because your value(s) was at risk.

Strengths

Accurate
Adaption
Administration
Adventurous
Advising
Ambitious
Analytical
Artistic
Assertive
Athletic
Authentic
Bookkeeping
Budgeting
Caring
Charming
Checking
Communication
Compassionate
Confident
Considerate
Coordination
Counseling
Courageous
Creative
Data analysis
Decisive
Dedicated
Delegation
Deliberate
Dependable
Detail-oriented
Determined
Disciplined
Educated
Empathetic
Energetic
Enthusiastic
Evaluation
Flexible
Focused
Honest
Idealistic
Implementation
Independent
Influence

Initiation
Innovation
Inspirational
Intelligent
Knowledgeable
Leader
Learning
Listening
Managing
Marketing
Motivated
Negotiation
Open-minded
Optimistic
Orderly
Organized
Patient
Peaceful
Planning
Preparation
Presentation
Prioritization
Problem-solving
Product development
Reporting
Research
Resolution
Resourceful
Respectful
Responsible
Sales
Spontaneous
Strategic
Supervision
Tactful
Teaching
Team building
Team-oriented
Technical skills
Thoughtful
Training
Trustworthy
Understanding
Uniting
Visionary

My Contributions To The World

Write down your contributions to the world. What will you do or say to contribute to the growth and development of your family, community, work culture and/or the world? Here are some questions you can ask yourself.

- How do you see yourself contributing to the world 1 - 2 years from now?
- How do you see yourself contributing to the world 5-10 years from now?
- What do you find exciting in or about the world?
- What angers you?
- What do you most want to teach or represent in this world?

Reflection - Purpose

After you have written your contributions, take time to reflect on them. Determine, what values are important as you contribute to the world? Why? What strengths can or will you use to help others? Are these values and strengths listed important? If not, go back and revise your values and strengths.

Before you create your purpose statement, review information you recorded in the previous steps. Do you need to make changes? Do you need to add additional information? Reflect on what stands out the most -what excites you the most? What are your most rewarding experiences?

Once you are finished, it is now time to create a draft purpose statement.

My Purpose Statement

It is now time to create a draft purpose statement. Use the guide below to help you create your draft statement on the next page, then create your final statement. Review the information you gathered to help you clarify your true life's purpose.

Once you have finalized your Purpose Statement, write your purpose statement, values, and strengths in the journal **Best Self** (Page 10). You can also write your statement on page 80 in this workbook.

A	B	C	D
Clarify what do you want to do? I/To (guide, inspire, support, create, etc.)	**Determine who you will help?** (community, children, leaders, etc.)	**Determine the impact?** (decreased health risk factors, increased confidence, etc.)	**Clarify how you will help others (your strengths)?** (coaching, teaching, blogging etc.)

SAMPLE STATEMENTS

* To cultivate the self-worth and net-worth of women around the world through public speaking and blogging.
* To inspire healthier communities by connecting people to real food.
* I will help emerging leaders activate their true potential through coaching and training.

My Motto Statement

A motto statement is how you want to live your life every day. It describes what you want to experience in life. Do you want to experience the beauty in life? Do you want to live each day as if it were your last?

A motto statement explains your character and how you see life.

Here are some example motto statements

- Every day, I will experience the beauty in life.
- I am a work in progress.
- I will live my best life every day.
- If I cannot find a way, I will make one.

Every day, think about how you are going to experience and activate your motto.

Once you have finalized your Motto Statement, write your statement in the journal **Best Self** (Page 10). You can also write your statement on page 80 in this workbook.

My Purpose and Motto Statements

MY PURPOSE

MY MOTTO

4 Guaranteed Strategies

to Change Undesired Behaviors

The fourth step to discover yourself is to review guaranteed strategies. These strategies are based on steps 1 and 2.

Life is a process of continuous change. Throughout our lives, we learn and re-learn things about ourselves, others, and our environment. This section summarizes strategies to help you attain desired goal. This section also reviews and provides examples of affirmations that can be repeated throughout the day.

After you determine your focus area (in step 5), use this section as a reference to create actions and daily habits in your journal **Best Self.**

Review the strategies listed below to help you reflect on what you want to start, stop, or continue to do to help you activate your best self.

Step 1 - Tune in and Turn on Strategies

Here is a summary of principles and practices to engage in to help you tune in and turn on.

- ☼ Practice mindfulness throughout the day
- ☼ Get into a habit taking deep breaths, throughout the day
- ☼ Meditate on a regular basis to clear your mind and focus on your life, clarifying your desires
- ☼ Throughout the day, focus on what you are grateful for, especially in a time of distress
- ☼ Focus on the journey, not just the destination

Step 2 - Building a Better Future Strategies

Take Control of Your Thoughts

Here is a summary of principles and practices to engage in to help you take control of your thoughts.

- ☼ Maintain a realistic evaluation of your emotions and how your emotions impact your work performance and relationships
- ☼ Admit your feelings and accept them
- ☼ Know your strengths and areas of development
- ☼ Accept yourself as you are; remind yourself that you are not perfect
- ☼ Seek encouragement (counselor/friend) if needed
- ☼ Engage in self-awareness activities such as books, retreats, counseling, etc.
- ☼ Ask for feedback from your peers
- ☼ Gain insights from mistakes
- ☼ Be committed to actively developing yourself
- ☼ Have a strong and positive sense of self-worth
- ☼ Revise self-defeating assumptions/beliefs with PAIA (Positive affirmations, intentions, and actions)
- ☼ Keep disruptive emotions and impulses under control by deep breathing, remaining gratitude focused and accepting yourself just as you are

Take Control of What You Say

Here is a summary of principles and practices to engage in to help you take control of what you say.

Listen Actively
- ☼ Listen non-judgmentally, practice empathy and compassion
- ☼ Listen for understanding rather than thinking about what you are going to say
- ☼ Allow your mind to be clear and quiet; enjoy what the other person is saying, soak in as much information as you can
- ☼ Reflect back your understanding of the message
    - o Restate basic ideas, facts
    - o Restate major ideas expressed including feelings
    - o Acknowledge the value of the speakers' issues and feelings
    - o Show appreciation for the speakers' effort and action
    - o Offer ideas or suggestions
    - o Ask for more information. Tell the speaker to give you more information (e.g., Can you tell me more? What happened next?)

Effectively Communicate with Others

☼ Communicate truthfully and honestly; follow through on what you say
☼ Recognize others communication styles
☼ Recognize and acknowledge generational and cultural differences in others
☼ Develop loyalty by showing interest, talking to people, and investing in relationships
☼ Provide clear rationale when options or actions change
☼ Seek out and use ideas, opinions, and insights from others (e.g., employees, people in the community, board of directors)
☼ Always follow up to determine if your message was understood
☼ Say thank-you for a job well done (send thank you cards)
☼ Expect that whatever you say will be shared. Be discrete at all times

Take Control of Your Physical Body

Here is a summary of principles and practices to engage in to help you take control of your physical body.

Diet

☼ Talk to your doctor or nutritionist about your specific needs
☼ Create a plan of what you eat on a daily basis at the beginning of each week (this can be done in the Journal Best Self)
☼ Increase your intake of fresh fruits and vegetables and decrease your intake of fatty and processed foods
☼ Eat smaller portioned meals
☼ Limit processed foods and foods made with white flour, white rice, and white sugar
☼ Stop eating before your body becomes full

Exercise

☼ Talk to your doctor or personal trainer
☼ Find creative ways to exercise (e.g., walking at lunch, wake up early and walk in your neighborhood, if you come to work early, walk around the building)
☼ When your exercise regime falls off track, quickly reflect and determine why. Ask yourself what do you need to do to continue a regular exercise regime (e.g., examine your schedule, attitude)?

Stress

☼ Accept the reality of frustration and discomfort

- ☼ Know that things may not go as planned at times
- ☼ Keep your challenge in perspective. Recognize there are always people in a tougher situation
- ☼ Pick a single, unproductive thing that's wasting your time and stop doing it today. Eliminate something else tomorrow
- ☼ Write down the cause of your stress and reflect on it
- ☼ Get organized and order your priorities professionally and personally
- ☼ Open up. The more others know about what's going on, the better they'll feel
- ☼ Recharge (e.g., spend time with family and loved ones, read a book, joke with a friend, take a short vacation)

Affirming What You Desire

Saying affirmations are important in your development. Affirmations are what you say, sing or speak on a daily basis. Affirmations are not about just repeating words or a phrase often. It is about saying or affirming something and having a feeling that represents what you say. The feeling that you have about something has to match what you are saying. If it doesn't, then you are not really creating what you desire; you are just merely saying words. So, throughout the day, make sure you have a feeling of what you are affirming, not what you do not desire.

Below is a list of affirmations related to the components in steps 1, 2 and 3. Affirmations should always be stated in positive terms. Affirmations should be reflective of what you desire; not what you don't desire.

- I am at peace.
- I love and accept myself.
- I am safe and always feel protected.
- I trust my inner being to lead me in the right path.
- I am free to be myself.
- I am responsible for my own Spiritual Growth.
- I grow in love every day.
- My strength comes from forgiveness of those who hurt me.
- My mind is at peace.
- I am open to receive love.
- I choose to let go because that is best for me.
- I am responsible for my feelings.
- I love myself just as I am.
- I am a capable human being.
- I am a skillful and artistic person.
- Taking risks is the path to growth.
- I focus on what brings me joy in my life.
- All is well.
- I am purpose driven.
- I relax and take care of my mind, body, and spirit.
- I will smoke less each day.
- I release all stress from my body.
- I do not fear being unhealthy because I know that I control my own body.
- I am always able to maintain my ideal weight.
- I am filled with energy to do all the daily activities in my life.
- I love and care for my body.
- I am surrounded by people who are loving and caring.
- I am the best friend I have.
- My children will benefit from my healthy changes.
- My family will benefit from my relaxing more.
- I attract a mate who is spiritual and kind, honest and giving.
- I deserve to love and be loved.
- I am ready for love to come to me.
- I do all I can every day to make a loving environment for all those around me, including myself.
- I am loving and accepting of others and this creates lasting friendships for me.
- I deserve to love and to be loved.
- I choose to let go because that is best for me.
- I am responsible for my feelings.

Think about what you are affirming in your life on a daily basis. Is it something you truly desire or represent? Are you affirming your fears?

Reflect on what you desire in your life right now. Write down affirmations that you desire to say, speak, or sing daily in your life that reflect your desires. Use the above affirmations to guide you.

5
Create a Plan of Action

Congratulations! You made it!!!

Now, it is time to create goals. In this workbook, you will clarify what you desire to continue to develop in and the action that needs to be taken to reach one or more desired goals. Creating goals will help you become more motivated and focused on what you want to achieve. It also reduces stress and improves your self-confidence and performance.

Plan

In this section you will:
- determine your focus area

- review sample action plan

- create goals –write your goals in the journal **Best Self (or in Appendix C)**

- review tips for success

Determine Your Focus Area

The first step to action planning is to determine your focus. What areas do you choose to focus on? What are high priority areas that you choose to work on?

You can determine your focus areas by identifying what you are satisfied with and what you need to work on. Before you complete the chart below, take time to reflect on your notes in the previous sections. You can create a goal based on your areas of improvement or you can create a goal to enhance your strengths.

Once you determine your strengths and areas of development reflect and think what are you willing to change? What's priority? What are you willing to work on right now regarding your strengths and areas of development? This will help you finalize what you really wish to work on. Here are some questions you may ask that may help you create your specific goals.

Tune in and turn on: Do you wish to engage in more practices to help you relax throughout the day? Do you crave to be more gratitude focused? Is there a principle that you desire to focus on developing?

Emotions: Is any part of your mind-set holding you back? Is there any part of the way you behave that upsets you? Have you accepted yourself as you are? Do you have a fear of something?

Social Interaction: Do you need to improve your interactions with others? How do you choose to be seen? Do you need to practice your active listening skills? Do you desire to learn to manage your anger? Is there a social principle that you wish to focus on developing?

Physical Body: Do you desire good health long into old age? Do you wish to eliminate unhealthy habits you have already fallen into? Do you desire to reduce stress? Do you desire to start exercising more?

Mental Aspiration: Do you wish to clarify your Life's purpose? Is there any knowledge you choose to acquire to help you in your life's purpose?

Peer Reflection - Optional

Before you complete the growth grid on the next page, get feedback about your areas of development from at least five **people you trust at work and/or in your personal life**. It is important to occasionally ask people you know and trust, for self-evaluations. You can just ask them a few simple questions such as:

What do you see as my strengths? What do I do well?

What do you see as my areas of development?

Activity
Review your strengths in step 3- Purpose. Are the strengths listed the same or similar as the strengths reported by your peers?

What do you feel I need to work on the most?

*You can download a peer reflection assessment at activateyourbest.com/reinvent (video series) to determine what your peers feel are your strengths and areas of growth.

Growth Grid

Based on all of the responses you previously recorded, determine what you are satisfied with and what you need to work on. Record your thoughts in the table below.

	I am satisfied with...	I need to work on...
Tune in and turn on		
Emotional		
Social interactions		
Physical body		
Other (e.g., savings, education, leadership skills)		

Continuous Improvement Areas:

Map It Out

Use the chart below to determine what is high priority and what is low priority. As a result, you can determine what you will focus on.

HIGH PRIORITY NEED IMPROVEMENT	HIGH PRIORITY STRENGTHS
LOW PRIORITY NEED IMPROVEMENT	LOW PRIORITY STRENGTHS

Create a Plan of Action

Once you have determined your priority areas, create 1 to 3 goals in the journal **Best Self Journal** at activateyourbest.com. Creating the development plan defines in detail what needs to be accomplished to further your development. The plan can be activated after you have created a clear visual of what you desire.

The next page shows an example of the action plan. There is a template of the action plan in the online guide at activateyourbest.com/reinvent. You can also complete the action plan in your journal, Best Self.

Action Plan Examples

Here is an example of an action plan. This plan provides a clear description of your goal and steps that will be taken to accomplish your goal. Use the Best Self Journal or Appendix C to write out your plan for action.

Goal	I intend to exercise, 30 minutes a day, at least four times a week and maintain a weigh of 140 pounds
Actions	<ul><li>Renew my membership at the gym</li><li>Start walking and doing aerobic exercises</li><li>Start working out for 10 minutes for 3 days a week</li><li>Each week, I will increase the time I work out by five minutes – I will do this until I am able to work out for 30 minutes a day, four days a week</li><li>Watch what I eat<ul><li>Increase my intake of fruits and vegetables and decrease my intake of processed foods and red meat by 50%</li></ul></li></ul>
Resources	Gym, personal trainers, books
Why is this important?	I desire to create a better future for myself and my family and improve my health
Timeline	July 1, 2021-Nov 1, 2021
Obstacles	I may get stressed at work and not go **Potential Solution:** Focus on keeping my body in great shape, do not let my emotions derail me

Outcome

What will the new me look like	**I am in great shape physically**
How will I measure success	I will measure success by the weight I loose and the energy that I have gained as a result of exercising regularly

Daily Activities

Affirmations	<ul><li>Losing weight comes natural to me</li><li>I take great care of my body</li><li>Every day I feel slimmer and lighter</li></ul>
Morning and evening activities*	**Each morning, I will:** Stretch my physical body, take deep breaths, meditate for 5 minutes, say affirmations, take vitamins and an energizer shake, and plan out what I will do for each day to achieve my goal **Before I go to sleep I will**: Take 5 deep breaths and focus on my affirmations *Morning – evening activities can also be recorded in the Best Self Journal page 11.

Let's review each component in the action plan.

Goals: When setting goals, they should be clearly written so there is clarity on the desired event or outcome. By creating goals, you can explore areas of interests that you have put off or activities that you have had difficulty accomplishing. Your goal statement is a statement of what you plan to achieve. Your goal statement should be:

- Expressed or written positively.
- Focused on dates, times, and amounts so that achievement can be measured.
- Clearly focus on what you what to attain.
- Written to avoid confusion.
- Realistic of what you wish to achieve. Goals may be set unrealistically because of:
    - other people (parents, media, society)
    - lack of a clear understanding of what you desire to achieve, or
    - setting goals too high
- Small and achievable; slightly out of your immediate reach.
- Rewarding to add some sort of benefit to your life.

Actions: Actions statements describe the specific actions you will take to meet your goal.

Resources: Resources show who or what can help you develop in this area such as a counselor, friends, books, or videos.

Why is this important: Why is this important helps you reflect on the benefits of accomplishing your goal.

Timeline: Timelines determines how long it will take you to complete this goal and important milestones. Make sure you write down when you will start and finish your plan. Usually, goals are:
- Short-term (0-6 months)
- Intermediate (6-1 year)
- Long-term (1 year or longer)

Obstacles: Obstacles show what may prevent you from reaching your goal and how you may conquer this obstacle.

Outcomes: Outcomes show the outcome of achieving your goal. Determine what you will be doing differently as a result of accomplishing this goal and how will you measure success.

Affirmations: Once you have incorporated a behavior, attitude, or way of thinking into your life, continue to say affirmations and think thoughts that will help you continue to activate your new way of life!

Morning and evening activities: Are there activities you do regularly, on a consistent basis, that will help you accomplish your goal? Determine what you will do mornings, evenings, weekly, and monthly, to develop in this area.

Tips for Success

Visualize Success

Once you determine your specific goal(s), write down your goal down and keep it where you will see it often. You can create a flowing visual image of what you desire in your mind. When you create a visual image, you create a feeling of what you desire to experience or a feeling of what the new you will look like after you have focused and made some changes. Be <u>passionate</u> about what you desire and feel yourself do what you intend to do or become.

For example, if your goal is to begin managing your mind talk, you can see yourself managing your mind talk by saying positive affirmations, surrounding yourself with positive people and creating affirmations such as:

- I let go of all hurts and past traumas
- I choose love
- I accept myself just as I am
- I release all thoughts of anger and resentment about myself and others

You can see yourself having and experiencing thoughts of love and honorable deeds. It is important to have flowing visuals throughout the day about your desires, especially when you arise in the morning and go to sleep at night. Have faith that you will achieve your goals, while being patient with yourself during this process. By doing this, you create a strong feeling of success and accomplishment in your mind.

It is important to create only 1-3 goals at a time. If you create more goals, you may begin to get unfocused and not follow through.

Take Action

After you complete your plan, take action. The most successful people in life have a specific routine that they follow daily to meet certain goals. Often, we get sidetracked, but that is fine. Just know that you need to get back on track as soon as possible. Develop a plan of what you need to do daily to attain your goals or change undesired behavior.

If you see you are getting off track, do not focus on failure; instead, focus on the improvements you made while you were on track and focus on next steps that you are going to take to get back on track. Sometimes, change and development does not come easy. There can be a continuous flow of challenges. But with persistence, you can accomplish whatever you choose to accomplish.

Here are some tips that will help you manage your time, manage crisis, and celebrate successes when carrying out your plan.

Manage Your Time
- Clarify your goals. Make sure it is truly what you want and intend to do
- Periodically analyze how you spend your time using a time log
- Set at least one objective a day and achieve it
- Focus on and complete what you start
- Resist impulses to focus on things that stray you away from your goal
- Focus your thoughts of achieving your goals in the mornings, when you wake up and at night before you go to sleep

Manage areas of growth
- Do not let any reoccurring crisis hinder you from achieving your goal
- Find the origin of the problem
- Learn to be proactive and not reactive
- Deal with a situation before it becomes a crisis
- Just take some time and take deep breaths

Celebrate successes
- Take time to reflect and think about the progress you have made, even if it is small
- Write down and reflect on your small accomplishments and milestones
- Reward yourself after you have successfully reached a goal or milestone

Know that through focus and endurance, you are on the path to creating a better you! As you evolve, your efforts at transformation may not be accomplished at the planned time. This is fine; however, you can reflect or re-write your goals to meet the current situation. Remember, we cannot control the constant changes in life. Moreover, once your goals are established, it is vital that you review and revise them as circumstances and conditions frequently fluctuate.

Act

Now it is time to Activate Your Best Self using our 90 Day Journal!

References

Allen, J. (1985). As a Man Thinketh. Brownlow Publishing: Forth Worth, Texas.

Ashby, M. A. (1997). Meditation, The Ancient Egyptian Path to Enlightenment. Kamit Publications: Brooklyn, New York.

Covey, S. (1990). The 7 Habits of Highly Effective People.

Goldburg, B. (1999). Alternative Medicine: The Definitive Guide. Future Medicine Publishing: Tiburon, CA.

Hay, L. (1999). You Can Heal Your Life. Hay House: Carlsbad, CA.

Weil, A. (1997). Eight Weeks to Optimal Health. Alfred Knopf: New York.

Wright, J. (1999). Reflexology and Accupressure. Octopus Publishing Group: Heron Quays, London.

Appendix A

Practicing Active Listening

This section helps you if you are having challenges listening actively. By listening actively, focus your full attention on the person who is speaking without judgment or other distractions.

Some ways to practice active listening are to:
- ☼ Restate basic ideas, facts
- ☼ Reflect the speaker's basic feelings
- ☼ Restate major ideas expressed including feelings
- ☼ Acknowledge the value of the speaker's issues and feelings
- ☼ Show appreciation for the speakers' effort and action
- ☼ Offer ideas or suggestions

You can practice developing your active listening skills by completing the chart below. The first column displays "what is said" and the second column shows an example of how you can respond to what was said.

Take time to reflect on the following examples of "what is said" and create potential responses. Also, reflect on your individual experiences. Write down examples of "what is said" and potential active listening responses.

What is Said	Active Listening Response
I am going to my mother's house next weekend but I am not sure I want to go	You seem hesitant about visiting your mother
I am not sure I can do this job; it is rather complicated	Are you saying . . .?

Appendix B

Practicing Assertive Communication

Communicating assertively is expressing feelings, thoughts, and desires directly without aggression. It recognizes your needs as well as the needs of others. When communicating assertively make sure you:

- Communicate with **integrity**. Make it about what you believe
- Recognize yes or no questions by responding with a yes/no answer
- Use "I" statements often.
  - o Say: "I don't agree with that idea", not, "your idea is stupid"
  - o Say: "I feel" statements rather than "I think" statements
- Be compassionate with others as you recognize that everyone is unique

Complete the following communication example. Think about a person you would like to be more assertive with. List the situation and then proceed on paper as if you were going to do so.

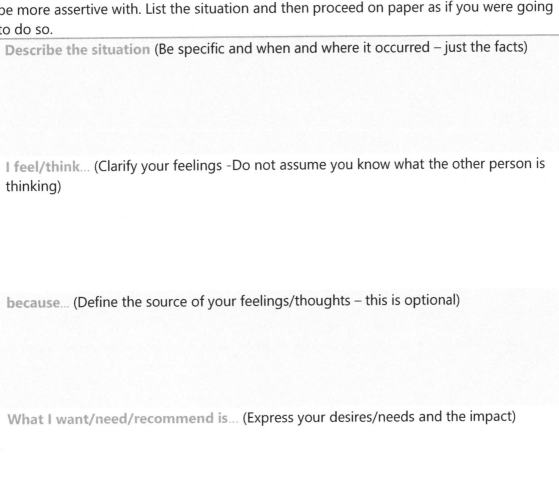

Describe the situation (Be specific and when and where it occurred – just the facts)

I feel/think... (Clarify your feelings -Do not assume you know what the other person is thinking)

because... (Define the source of your feelings/thoughts – this is optional)

What I want/need/recommend is... (Express your desires/needs and the impact)

Appendix C – Action Plan

Action Plan

Goal	
Actions	
Resources	
Why is this important?	
Timeline	
Obstacles	

Outcome

What will the new me look like	
How will I measure success	

Daily Activities

Affirmations	
Morning and evening activities*	

Action Plan

Goal	
Actions	
Resources	
Why is this important?	
Timeline	
Obstacles	

Outcome

What will the new me look like	
How will I measure success	

Daily Activities

Affirmations	
Morning and evening activities*	

Additional Notes

About the Author

Dr. Jessica Blalock is an organizational psychologist, executive coach, and author. She has delivered innovative services and products to enhance leadership, staff development and program processes and performance. She earned her Ph.D. in Psychology, with a focus in Applied Psychology, from the University of Tennessee. She has more than 15 years of experience and has worked nationally and internationally with a variety of clients including government, non-profit, private, education, utilities, and financial. Dr. Blalock has worked with Fortune 500, mid-sized and small organizations domestically and international.

Additional Products by the Author

Gratitude Journal, Jessica Blalock, Ph.D.
activateyourbest.com/shop

Best Self, Jessica Blalock, Ph.D.
activateyourbest.com/shop

Discover Yourself for Youth, Jessica Blalock, Ph.D.
activateyourbest.com/shop

At My Best, Jessica Blalock, Ph.D.
activateyourbest.com/shop

Made in United States
North Haven, CT
01 May 2022